	DATE DUE		

MARTIAN FOSSILS ON EARTH?

THE STORY OF METEORITE ALH 84001

FRED BORTZ

THE
MILLBROOK
PRESS

BROOKFIELD,
CONNECTICUT

For my daughter, Rosalie,
and all the discoveries that await her.

Photographs courtesy of: NASA: pp. 6, 9, 10, 14, 16 (top), 16-17, 20, 23, 28, 42, 44 (both), 46, 51 (bottom), 52, 60, 62, 63 (both); Smithsonian Astrophysical Observatory/Ghislaine Crozaz: p. 12; National Optical Astronomy Observatories: p. 36; D. S. McKay, et. al., "Search for Past Life on Mars: Possible Relic Biogenic Activity in Martian Meteorite ALH84001," Science, vol. 273, pp. 924-930, 16 August 1996, © American Association for the Advancement of Science: pp. 34, 38 (both, false color produced by Craig Schwendt), 39, 40 (both); © Susan A. Kitchens www.auntialias.com: p. 48 (both); Geological Survey of Canada (photo number GSC 1994-760 F): p. 51 (top). Computer-generated illustration on p. 25 by Fred Bortz.

Library of Congress Cataloging-in-Publication Data
Bortz, Alfred B.
Martian fossils on earth? : the story of meteorite ALH 84001 / by Fred Bortz.
p.   cm.
Includes bibliographical references and index.
Summary: Discusses the study of a meteorite found in Antarctica in 1984 and why it is thought to come from Mars, examining how the scientific process works.
ISBN 0-7613-0270-0 (lib. bdg.)
1. Meteorites–Antarctica–Juvenile literature. 2. Mars (Planet)–Juvenile literature. 3. Fossils–Juvenile literature. [1. Meteorites. 2. Mars (Planet) 3. Life on other planets.] I. Title
QB755.2.B67   1997   97-6190
523.5'1–dc21   CIP   AC

Published by The Millbrook Press, Inc.
2 Old New Milford Road
Brookfield, Connecticut 06804

CONTENTS

MARTIAN FOSSILS ON EARTH?

METEORITE ALH 84001

1

WHY ARE SCIENTISTS SO EXCITED ABOUT A ROCK?

Because scientists love the excitement of discovery, they sometimes love the search for answers even more than the answers themselves. That is why they are so excited about a rock. Deep within this rock are structures and substances that will allow scientists to explore one of the most intriguing questions of all time:

*T*he rock is known as meteorite ALH 84001. It is about the size and shape of a potato and weighs 1.94 kilograms (about 4 pounds). A meteorite is a rock that fell to Earth from space.

Meteorite ALH 84001 landed in the Allan Hills area of Antarctica about 13,000 years ago. It was discovered in December 1984 by the scientists of the Antarctic Search for Meteorites (ANSMET) project, led by William Cassidy.

ANSMET scientists have found about 7,000 meteorites since the project began in 1976. After each meteorite-hunting season, the ANSMET scientists send their extraterrestrial rock collection to the Lyndon B. Johnson Space Center (JSC) in Houston, Texas. There, the meteorites are numbered and carefully cut into pieces, which are sent to scientists all over the world for study. ALH 84001 was the most interesting and unusual item in the Allan Hills 1984–1985 rock collection. The meteorite's name means "Allan Hills, 1984–1985 season, number 001."

Some meteorites come from wandering chunks of rock left over from the formation of Earth and other planets of the solar system. Other meteorites appear to be fragments of Moon-sized bodies that formed and then were broken apart. Like the planets, meteorites travel at very high speeds around the sun in paths called orbits. If a rock's orbit brings it near Earth, it may enter Earth's atmosphere and collide with our planet.

Just as water slows your body when you dive into a swimming pool, the atmosphere slows the rock. Scientists call the force that slows your body, or the rock, friction. The friction transforms the rock's energy of motion into heat. The rock begins to melt, and the atmosphere begins to glow, forming a streak of light that crosses the sky. When we on Earth see the glow, we call it a meteor, or a "shooting star" (although it has nothing to do with stars).

Most meteors are small or are made of light materials. These burn up entirely when they enter the atmosphere, leaving only vapor and bits of dust. A few meteor-causing bodies are large and fall to the ground as meteorites.

How do scientists recognize a meteorite? First, the outside of a meteorite shows signs of its fiery trip through the atmosphere. It is often oddly shaped, and its surface is smooth or glassy. Second, the rock is out of place. It is made of minerals unlike the other rocks around it.

Sometimes the original meteorite is so huge that it leaves a visible crater on Earth. About 10,000 years ago, a large rock composed mainly of iron and nickel struck the ground about 50 kilometers (30 miles) east of the present-day city of Flagstaff, Arizona. It blasted out a huge hole, about 1 kilometer (more than half a mile) across. It is commonly called "Meteor Crater," although its official name is the Barringer Meteorite Crater. ⬇ Many nickel-iron meteorites have been collected from that site.

Scientists classify each meteorite as a member of a family, according to its physical appearance and mineral makeup. A meteorite family is often named after the location where the first such meteorite is found.

ALH 84001 is a shergottite meteorite. The first known shergottite meteorite fell in Shergotty, India, on August 25, 1865. ANSMET scientists have since found many more shergottite meteorites, including the small, black, crusty one pictured here, designated QUE 94201. It was found in the Queen Alexandra Range during the Antarctic summer of 1994–1995.

A meteorite that fell and killed an unfortunate dog in Nakhla, Egypt, on June 28, 1911, was the first to be classified as nakhlite. Another fell in Chassigny, France, on October 3, 1815, and was designated chassignite. Later, other nakhlite meteorites were found in Lafayette, Indiana, in 1931, and in Governador Valadares, Brazil, in 1958. Together, the shergottite, nakhlite, and chassignite meteorites are known as SNC meteorites.

Meteorite ALH 84001 was first identified incorrectly as a rare form of another mineral family—the diogenites. In 1993, meteoriticist (meteorite scientist) David Mittlefehldt caught the error. He announced that meteorite ALH 84001 was the tenth known member of the SNC class. Two other SNC meteorites were found in 1995. Those dozen rocks are very special indeed, for scientists now believe that the SNC meteorites are pieces of the planet Mars.

On August 7, 1996, meteorite ALH 84001 became the most famous rock on Earth. That day, a team of scientists led by David S. McKay of JSC made an astounding announcement. They believed that meteorite ALH 84001 contained chemical evidence and fossils of ancient Martian microbes. Life may have begun on Mars at about the same time as on Earth!

2

HOW WAS METEORITE ALH84001 DISCOVERED?

Who would want to live for months in Antarctica, where it snows even in the summertime? Thousands of scientists from around the world, that's who! Among them are the researchers of the Antarctic Search for Meteorites (ANSMET) project. Although meteorites are no more likely to fall on Antarctica than on other places, they are much easier to find there. And the meteorites found in Antarctica are in better condition.

In December, as the Antarctic summer begins, ANSMET scientists mount their snowmobiles and go looking for dark rocks standing out against the ice. ↓ When they find one, they examine it carefully. If it is similar to normal Antarctic rocks, they leave it alone. It probably came loose from some nearby hillside. It almost surely moved with the slowly flowing Antarctic ice sheet for hundreds or thousands of years until, by chance, it became visible in an area swept free of snow by a steady Antarctic wind.

But if the rock is different, then the scientists wonder where it came from.

Was it put there by a person? No. The only people who have ever inhabited Antarctica live and work in scientific research stations.

Was it put there by an animal? No. The only animals that spend part of their lives on land in Antarctica are seals, penguins, and a few other creatures that are never far from the shore of the Antarctic Ocean. No other animals have lived on that frozen continent for millions of years.

So what's left? Did it fall from the sky? If the rock has an odd shape and a glassy surface, it almost surely did just that. It is probably a meteorite.

The ice of Antarctica makes it easier to find meteorites, and the climate there protects them. In other parts of the world, weather conditions, such as rain and wind, can change the surface of the meteorite. The changing seasons can also damage it. In warm months, water finds its way into cracks in the rock. In winter, the water turns to ice and expands, often causing the rock to break into pieces. After many years of weathering—wind and rain, freezing and thawing—the meteorite breaks down and becomes part of the soil. Besides damaging the surface of a meteorite, liquid water can also affect the interior. It often carries other substances into cracks, where they deposit chemicals.

Only in Antarctica can a meteorite be exposed to the weather for thousands of years without much damage. After meteorite ALH 84001 landed about 13,000 years ago, the Antarctic climate and a protective cover of snow preserved it until ANSMET researcher Roberta Score noticed it.

There's another reason that ANSMET researchers happily bundle up to go meteorite hunting in this always-frigid place. If they find another piece of Mars, they want their prize to be free of pollution from human-made chemicals. Meteorite ALH 84001

shows signs of chemical reactions. Within its cracks, scientists found small, chemically deposited globules (round masses) of carbonate minerals. ⬆ Because it has been on solid Antarctic ice ever since it landed on Earth, scientists believe that the carbonate globules probably formed on Mars.

The meteorite also contains chemicals called polycyclic aromatic hydrocarbons (PAHs) that may be a sign of life. If it had been discovered any other place on earth, its PAHs might have come from vegetation or air pollution. But in Antarctica, except along the coastline, no vegetation grows, and its air is the purest and cleanest on Earth.

Do the PAHs in ALH 84001 mean that it once contained life? You'll discover more about that question later. But you can be certain that it is easier to answer the question with an Antarctic meteorite than with one found most anywhere else in the world.

3

HOW CAN WE TELL THAT THIS METEORITE COMES FROM MARS?

To study a meteorite, scientists usually cut it into many pieces, then examine each piece. Meteorite ALH 84001 was divided into many pieces. It was photographed after each cut. Each piece was labeled and measured so scientists knew where it came from in the original meteorite.

In some pictures of meteorites, you can see rulers marked in centimeters. In others you can see little cubes. ↑ The cubes are one centimeter (0.39 inch) on a side. You can see the same cubes in pictures of rocks returned by Apollo astronauts from the Moon. Each of the cube's six sides is marked with a letter: T, B, N, E, S, and W for top, bottom, north, east, south, and west.

The cube is an indication of the size of the rock you are viewing in a photograph. The actual directions are not important for meteorites, since weather or earth and ice movements constantly change meteorites' positions from the time they fall until the time they are discovered. Still, the cube markings can help you understand photographs of the same meteorite from different angles.

After meteorites are cut, their pieces go to meteoriticists in many different laboratories around the world. Each laboratory has its own special equipment. Some meteoriticists study the gases that are trapped inside the meteorite. The gases can sometimes reveal interesting facts about the history of a meteorite. For the SNC meteorites, the gases are often the strongest evidence that those rocks were once part of the planet Mars.

In 1976, two United States Viking spacecraft landed on Mars. They sent back detailed measurements of the gases of the Martian atmosphere. From Earth-based measurements, scientists already knew that the air on Mars was mainly carbon dioxide. The Viking measurements told them how much of the Martian atmosphere was nitrogen, neon, krypton, xenon, and other gases.

In 1983, scientists studying meteorite EETA 79001 found that its trapped gases matched the Viking measurements of the atmosphere of Mars. Since then, scientists have measured trapped gases in most SNC meteorites, and have found traces of Martian air.

Before the trapped-gas studies, scientists had another reason to believe that the SNC rocks did not originally come from Earth. Although those rocks contain minerals that are similar to Earth's, they have one very important distinction. The oxygen in the minerals is different.

Every substance is made out of atoms. The center of an atom, called the nucleus, is made up of two kinds of tiny particles called protons and neutrons. Protons and neutrons weigh just about the same amount. (Neutrons are slightly heavier.) Every oxygen atom has eight protons. Most oxygen atoms also have eight neutrons, but some have nine or ten.

These three different forms of oxygen are called "isotopes," and scientists distinguish them by their total number of protons and neutrons: O^{16}, O^{17}, or O^{18}. When it comes to chemical reactions, like burning or forming minerals, all three isotopes behave in the same way, but the products of those chemical reactions, like the oxygen atoms that go into them, have slightly different weights.

Just as Martian air can be identified by the mixture of gases in it, SNC meteorites can be identified by their mixture of oxygen isotopes, which is quite different from the mixture of oxygen isotopes in the minerals of Earth. It is also quite different from the mixture of oxygen isotopes in other families of meteorites.

Scientists are a very cautious group. Because of the mixtures of oxygen isotopes in the SNC meteorites, they will say *there is strong evidence* or they will say they *believe* that the rocks all come from the same "parent body," and that the parent body is not Earth. Because of the trapped-gas measurements, they will say that the parent body *is probably* Mars.

Even those who believe most strongly are not ready to say they *know* that the SNC meteorites are Martian. They must first study known Martian rocks with equipment here on Earth. In a few years, a spacecraft will visit Mars and bring back a load of stones and soil. Then we may have some answers about the SNC meteorites and about Martian fossils on Earth.

A mission to Mars will provide a number of answers, but no doubt it will also give scientists many more questions!

THE PLANET MARS

4

WHERE ON MARS DID ALH84001 COME FROM, AND HOW DID IT GET TO EARTH?

The solar system can be a violent place. It is full of objects made of rock, metal, ice, or frozen gases. The objects have very different shapes and sizes, and each one whizzes around in its own orbit around the Sun. Sometimes they smash into one another.

When two of these hunks or chunks meet at low velocity, they may end up in orbits close to each other. After many low-velocity collisions, a lot of material may collect in one area. Gradually the force of gravity pulls that collection together into one large body. Scientists believe that may be how the planets formed. Over a very long time, a few large collections came together to form the planets and their moons.

After these large bodies were formed, many smaller pieces were left over, and they still travel around the Sun in long looping paths.

Other smaller pieces may have resulted from violent collisions of Moon-sized bodies. Some are large enough to be called comets or asteroids, but most are much smaller.

The planets and their moons formed about 4.6 billion years ago. Since then, a steady rain of smaller objects has fallen onto them as meteorites. Most meteorites are small, but sometimes a larger piece of wandering rock crashes into a planet or moon. A collision like that leaves its mark, usually a crater like the Meteor Crater in Arizona or like the ones in this photo ➡ of the Martian surface.

Meteorite ALH 84001 began its journey toward Earth with a powerful event—most likely a meteorite impact—that blasted it into space. To launch a chunk of rock away from a planet and into orbit around the Sun, the meteorite impact had to be powerful enough to leave behind a large crater.

Scientist Nadine Barlow has a computer catalog of information about thousands of Martian craters. As other scientists determined the history of meteorite ALH 84001, she searched her catalog for likely places that could have been its original location on Mars. Although she is still not completely certain, she identifies the oval crater in this picture as a good candidate.

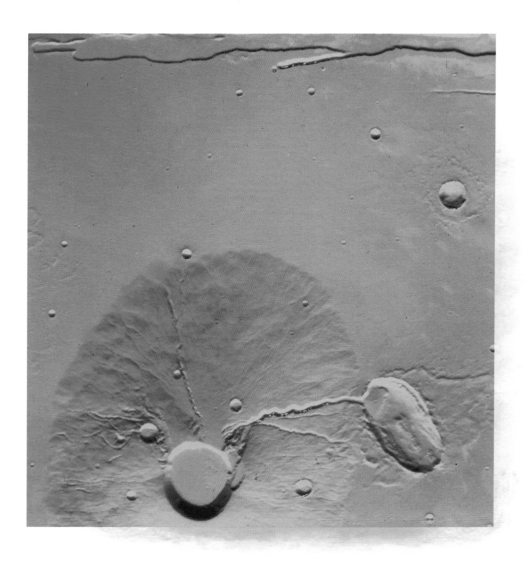

She has many reasons for her choice. One reason is that for an incoming body to make an oval-shaped crater instead of a circular one, it must nearly skim across the surface of the planet. A skimming impact is much more likely to knock part of the planet into space than one that comes from more directly overhead.

Other reasons derive from scientific measurements of meteorite ALH 84001 and of Mars. We have a good idea of how long ago the rock formed (about 4.5 billion years ago), how long it spent in space before it finally fell to Earth (about 16 million years), and how long it lay on the ice before it was found (about 13,000 years).

We also have a good idea of when and where its carbonate globules formed (about 3.6 billion years ago on Mars). We know that those globules formed in cracks in the rock, and that those cracks probably resulted from an earlier impact. We also know those globules mean that the rock was often exposed to liquid water.

The Martian surface around the oval crater is among the oldest regions on the planet, probably about 4.5 billion years old. The oval crater is near the edge of a severely weathered crater, which is probably about the same age as the globules. If meteorite ALH 84001 came from there, the impact that made the old crater probably made the cracks where the globules are now.

The oval crater has sharp edges, and it has not been hit by other meteorites. Those facts indicate that it was created recently. In a planet whose age is measured in billions of years, 16 million years ago—the time when ALH 84001 began its journey toward Earth—is very recent indeed. In comparison to human age, if Mars were twelve years old, then the impact that created the crater would have taken place only about two weeks ago.

Finally, you can see that the crater lies on what appears to be an ancient Martian riverbed. Scientists believe that Mars once had a much warmer climate and plenty of flowing water, just what was needed to create carbonate deposits in cracks in its rocks.

The impact that sent us meteorite ALH 84001 also launched many other bits and pieces of Mars into orbit. Each of those objects followed its own path around the Sun, completing a circuit in about two years.

For meteorite ALH 84001 and all the other pieces of Mars, each trip around the Sun was a little different from the one before. If the meteorite happened to collide with another wandering rock, both of them would change speed and direction. Once in every orbit, it would overtake Jupiter, like a fast runner passing a slower one in the neighboring lane of a racetrack. The gravity of Jupiter, the giant of the solar system, would give the rock a tug, causing its orbit to change again. The same thing happened every time Earth overtook the meteorite.

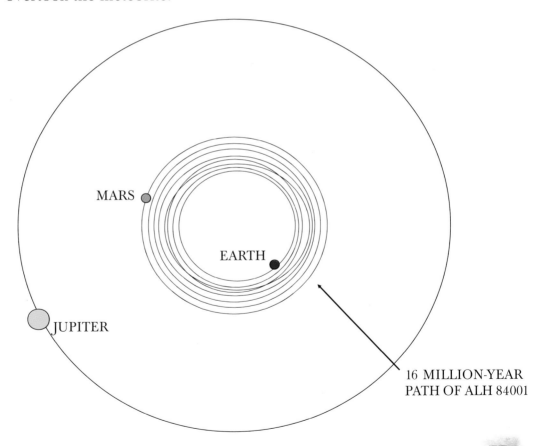

MARS

EARTH

JUPITER

16 MILLION-YEAR
PATH OF ALH 84001

By pure chance, these encounters with asteroids, other chunks of rock, and the neighboring planets put ALH 84001 on a path toward Earth.

Over millions of years, thousands of impacts have blasted millions of pieces of Mars into space. They have gone off in all directions, and their orbits are always changing. Without doubt, some of them are heading for our part of the solar system right now. Every year, some of these may fall to Earth. Most will never be found. Occasionally one may kill an Egyptian dog, or another may drop unnoticed onto the Antarctic ice to be discovered thousands of years later.

Each of them has a story to reveal to us. When we find them, it is important for us to know what questions to ask and how to seek the answers.

5

WHAT IS METEORITE ALH 84001 MADE OF?

A simple piece of rock can tell an amazing story—if you know how to read it. The story is written in the language of mineralogy and geochemistry, and it is read through scientific observation and measurement.

Parts of the language are easy to read. As a meteorite makes its blazing grand entrance through Earth's atmosphere, its outer surface melts, then quickly hardens into a glassy black "fusion crust." In this picture of a split-open meteorite ALH 84001, you can easily see the fusion crust on the upper and left-hand surfaces.

The meteorite may shatter in the atmosphere or on impact with Earth's surface. Or, Earth's natural forces (such as weather or moving ice sheets) may destroy part of its crust. Still, some smooth black coating remains on most meteorites, quietly identifying itself to a scientist who studies it carefully or almost shouting out, "I am a meteorite!" to any ANSMET scientist who spots it against a background of snow and ice.

To read the rest of the story, scientists begin by identifying the minerals inside the meteorite. Most meteorites belong to a number of common types, and a trained meteoriticist usually recognizes them immediately. The ANSMET scientists knew right away that meteorite ALH 84001 was not one of those types.

Although they could tell their rock was unusual, the scientists still misread the most important part of its mineralogical story, the part that proclaimed, "I was born on Mars!" Unfortunately that message was written in an ancient language spelled out in the chemical composition of volcanic, or igneous, rock.

Except for its carbonate globules, meteorite ALH 84001 is an igneous rock. It probably formed in the same way as the newborn basalt left behind by the slowly flowing stream of lava from the Hawaiian volcano Kilauea. Beneath the volcano is a huge chamber of hot, liquid rock known as magma. Mars, like Earth, once had many magma chambers within it. The collisions that formed the planets released so much energy that the planets' interiors were hot enough to melt rock.

Because Mars was barely half as large as Earth from one side to the other, its core cooled much faster. As far as we know, very little new igneous rock is now forming on Mars. But 4.5 billion years ago, when both Earth and Mars were young, vast areas of both planets were covered with flowing rivers of lava that quickly hardened into igneous rock. That process diminished over billions of years on both planets, although it continues in volcanic regions of Earth today.

Inside the magma chambers, heavy minerals sank toward the planets' centers, and lighter ones floated on top. As the magma oozed out, more heavy minerals and fewer lighter ones were left behind. Younger igneous rocks were different from older ones, but in a predictable way.

Of all the meteorites now known to be from Mars, ALH 84001 is by far the oldest. The others are younger by nearly 3 billion to more than 4 billion years. Their differences are so great that when meteoriticists first analyzed ALH 84001, they didn't see a match to the others of the SNC class. Instead, they identified it as an unusual member of another class of meteorites, known as diogenites.

For nine years, the world's most famous rock sat in Houston, misidentified. Then Donald Mittlefehldt recognized important similarities between its minerals and those of its much younger cousins. Additional study, including oxygen-isotope analysis, demonstrated that it had come from the same parent body as the SNCs. More than that, the age of its igneous minerals was greater than those in any Martian rock ever measured.

6

HOW DO WE KNOW THE AGE AND HISTORY OF ALH84001?

How can scientists say so much about the history of meteorite ALH 84001? They used clues in its chemical makeup and its physical structure.

RADIOACTIVE DATING

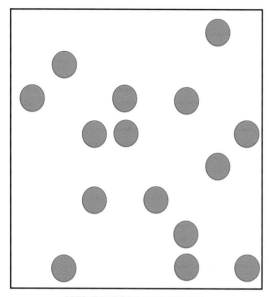

NEWLY FORMED ROCK

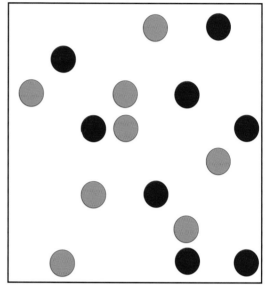

AFTER ONE HALF-LIFE

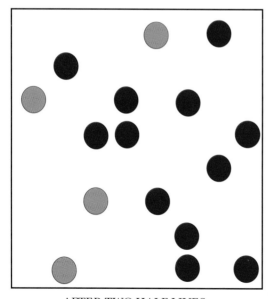

AFTER TWO HALF-LIVES

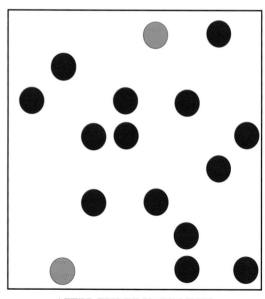

AFTER THREE HALF-LIVES

They use a technique called radioactive dating ◀▥ to determine the age when it first formed.

Every substance on Earth is made of atoms. Atoms almost never change from one element into another, but occasionally such a transformation does occur. We call that transformation "radioactive decay." Like oxygen, the atoms of most elements can exist in the form of several different isotopes with different numbers of neutrons. Some isotopes are radioactive and some are not.

We can predict that every radioactive atom will decay at some time in the future. Unfortunately, we can't forecast when a particular atom's time will come. Still, we can predict something that is useful. We can say that over a certain period of time, half of those atoms will decay. That period is called its "half-life."

In the diagram, the original radioactive atoms (scientists call these the "parents") are red, and the atoms they become after decay (called the "daughters") are blue. Suppose that when the rock crystallizes from magma, it has lots of red atoms and no blue ones. After one half-life, only half of the red atoms remain, and there is an equal number of blue ones.

In the next half-life, half of the remaining reds decay, leaving only one-fourth of the original number. After three half-lives, only one-eighth of the original reds are left. For every one of those, there are now seven blues.

By measuring the number of reds and blues, scientists can determine how long ago the rock formed. Of course, the parent and daughter atoms aren't really red and blue. They may be common elements like potassium and argon, or perhaps rarer ones like samarium and neodymium. Depending on the kinds of minerals in the rock and the approximate age of the event they are dating, scientists know which parent-daughter combinations are most useful for their purpose.

The most reliable measurements of ALH 84001 revealed that the meteorite had formed as an igneous rock about 4.5 billion years ago, or only 100 million years after the formation of the solar system! Its age was greater than that of any Martian rock ever measured.

When the rock first formed, it contained only high-temperature minerals from the magma. It was solid, without cracks. Carbonate minerals form at much lower temperatures than magma. The carbonate globules of meteorite ALH 84001, shown here, would never have formed if something had not cracked the rock, allowing lower-temperature fluids to seep in.

That something was most likely a meteorite impact. Scientists see evidence of that impact in the jumbled crystal structure of some of the minerals in the rock. Its appearance resembles the patterns found in rocks on Earth near impact craters or underground nuclear

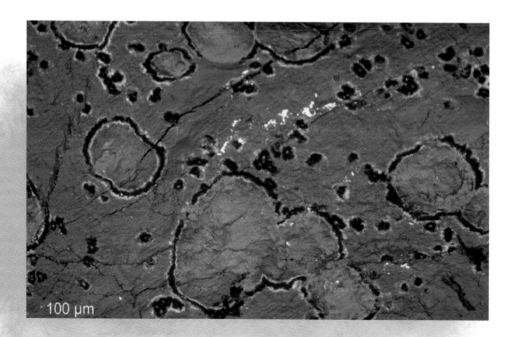

100 µm

explosions. How much later did that impact occur? Radioactive dating suggests that it occurred about 3.8 billion years ago, or about 700 million years after the rock first formed.

Perhaps the flowing water of an ancient Martian river, full of dissolved carbon dioxide from the Martian atmosphere, bathed the newly formed cracks. Perhaps that stream also carried dissolved minerals from other rocks along its path. Conditions like that would explain the formation of pancake-shaped globules of carbonate on the walls of many of the tiny fractures. Watery, protected conditions like that would also provide a cozy environment where Martian bacteria might thrive.

Many scientists think that is exactly how those globules formed 3.6 billion years ago (according to radioactive dating measurements of the carbonates), not long after the cracks opened up. Others disagree and argue that the carbonates formed under different conditions at a temperature that was too hot to permit life.

If bacteria did live there, they almost surely would have left behind chemical evidence of their life processes and tiny fossil structures in the globules. Is that what scientists have found in meteorite ALH 84001?

Those bacteria, if that's what they were, were dead for billions of years before the next impact launched them into space, where they orbited the Sun on a tiny fragment of their home planet for 16 million years. Again, we use radioactivity to measure the time that meteorite ALH 84001 spent in space. This time, however, it is not the decay of radioactive atoms. Instead it is their creation.

As the rock orbited the Sun, it was bombarded by a steady stream of high-energy particles known as the solar wind. In this

picture taken during a total solar eclipse, ⬆ you can see the corona surrounding the Sun and the solar flares leaping into space. That is where the solar wind begins.

Our planet's magnetic field protects us from this stream of particles, but meteorite ALH 84001 was exposed to its full force as it orbited between Mars and Earth. When the solar particles struck its surface, they transformed some of its non-radioactive atoms into their radioactive cousins. The longer the rock orbited, the more of those radioactive atoms it gained.

Once the meteorite landed in Antarctica where it was no longer exposed to the solar wind, its radioactivity began to drop again. By measuring the radioactivity of several different elements, scientists determined that it had been on the ice for thirteen thousand years before the ANSMET team discovered it. From that information, they could determine how high its level of radioactivity had been when it first landed. To build up to that level, meteorite ALH 84001 must have spent 16 million years in space.

7

DID MARTIAN MICROBES MAKE THESE CHEMICALS AND CRYSTALS?

If ancient Martian bacteria
lived anywhere inside meteorite
ALH 84001, the place to look
for them is in and near the
carbonate globules.

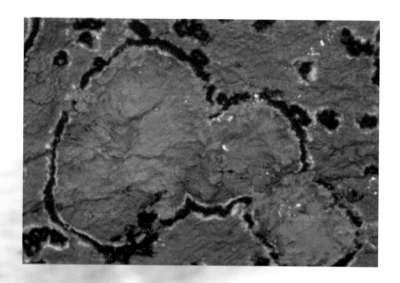

This highly magnified image shows a typical globule. ⬆ Because the image is produced by a technique called electron backscattering instead of light, its colors had to be created artificially.

Scientists often use false or intensified colors like these to emphasize differences between measurements. In this case, the colors are similar to those of actual globules, but more intense. The main body of the pancake-shaped globule, shown in orange, is composed of a magnesium- and iron-containing carbonate. It is about as large across as a human hair.

Separating the globule from the green mineral (called orthopyroxene) that makes up most of the meteorite are two rims. The inner black rim is mainly a carbonate of magnesium; it contains very little iron. The outer white rim contains less magnesium and is rich in iron. Most of that iron is in the form of a carbonate compound; but some of it is in iron sulfide or in magnetite, a compound of iron and oxygen known for its magnetic properties. (The first known magnets, lodestones, were small chunks of magnetite.)

Scientists have many possible explanations for the rims. Among those possibilities is bacterial activity. Some "magnetotactic" bacteria on Earth make tiny crystals of magnetite, which enable them to move along the "lines of force" of our planet's magnetic field. When scientists examined the white rims in ALH 84001 with a powerful magnifying machine called a transmission electron microscope (TEM), they discovered magnetite grains (the darkest regions in this TEM image ⬇) that were similar in size and shape to those made by Earth's magnetotactic microbes.

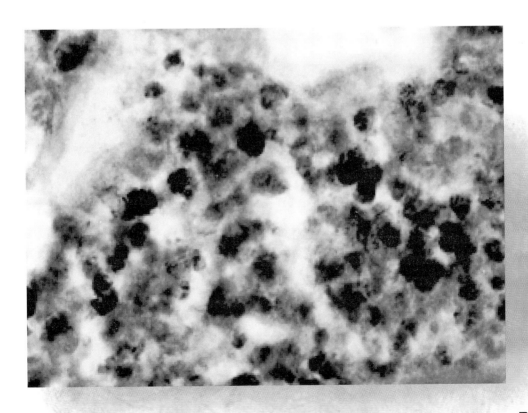

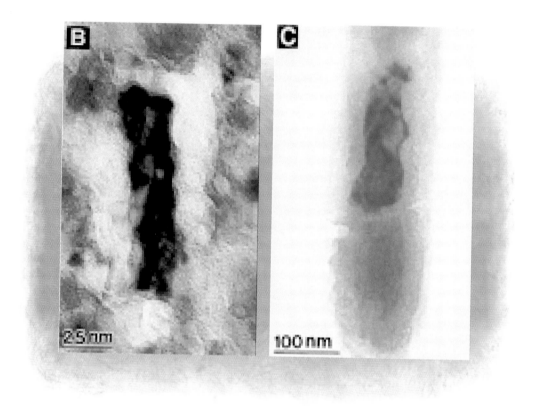

25 nm

100 nm

The iron sulfide in those white rims also suggests the possibility of life. The TEM image ⬆ on the left is a highly magnified crystal of iron sulfide from the meteroite, probably in a form known as greigite. On the right is a TEM image of a microbe within a root cell from Earth's soil with a similarly shaped greigite core. The magnifications are different; the tiny bit of Martian iron sulfide is actually about half the size of the bacterium's greigite core. If bacteria produced the magnetite and greigite in the white rims of the globules, then those tiny crystals might be called "chemical fossils."

Other chemical evidence of possible ancient life in ALH 84001 comes from measurements of a group of compounds known as polycyclic aromatic hydrocarbons, or PAHs. In the meteorite, the PAHs are concentrated in the areas of the globules.

PAHs are common on Earth. They can be produced by the decay of dead organisms or by industrial processes. You may be familiar with the smell of one PAH, naphthalene, which is the main ingredient in mothballs.

PAHs are also common in other meteorites that are known to be lifeless. So why do scientists think the PAHs in meteorite ALH 84001 mean that it once contained microscopic living creatures? Simply put, of all the possible PAHs, the meteorite seems to favor only a few types. Other meteorites contain a much broader mixture of PAHs. Scientists know of no processes, outside of life, that favor a few PAHs over all others.

Still, scientists are careful not to jump to conclusions about PAHs and life in ALH 84001. Early studies of meteorite EETA 79001 found PAHs that seemed to point to life on Mars. Unfortunately, more careful studies showed that those PAHs came from earthly contamination of the meteorite after it was brought back from the Antarctic. Because of that embarrassing incident, the scientists studying ALH 84001 have been extremely careful in their analysis of PAHs. The first team to study it noted that its surface was at least as clean of PAHs as any previously studied rock. At every step, scientists followed careful anticontamination procedures.

When they finally measured the PAHs, they found few on the outside and increasing amounts as they went farther into the meteorite. If the PAHs had come from Antarctica or anywhere else on Earth, you would expect them to be more concentrated on the surface than inside. It is almost certain that the PAHs in meteorite ALH 84001 formed on Mars.

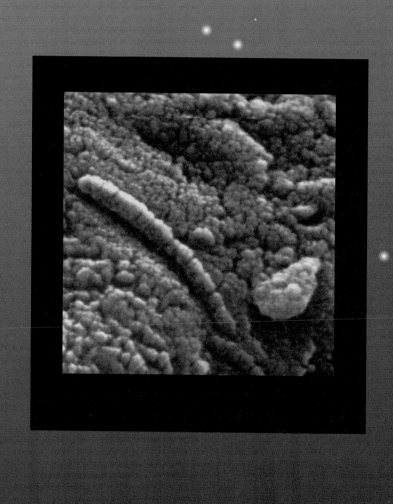

8

DID MARTIAN MICROBES LOOK LIKE THIS?

After finding possible life-induced chemical products in meteorite ALH 84001–PAHs, magnetite, and tiny elongated crystals that are probably greigite–what do scientists look for next?

They look for as much additional evidence as they can find, including structures in the rock that resemble fossils of bacteria on Earth. Who can blame them for being excited when their scanning electron microscope image of a carbonate globule ← revealed this tiny wormlike shape?

When a scientific discovery is as exciting as possible life on Mars, scientists have to be careful not to jump to conclusions. Although life is one possible explanation for the presence of PAHs, magnetite, and greigite, other explanations must also be considered. Could natural processes, other than life, create structures like that "worm"? Possibly. Nature often surprises us with orderly forms that are difficult to explain.

Were scientists too eager to see microscopic bacteria after they discovered chemicals that resembled the products of living organisms? Or should they have been searching for different ways those chemicals could have gotten there? The "worm" is the most dra-

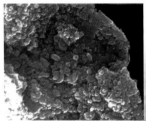

matic image of a possible bacterial fossil, but images like these ⬅ are even more persuasive to most scientists. Bacteria live in colonies. These micrographs show possible colonies of egg-shaped and tube-shaped forms on the surface of a carbonate globule. The image on the left is a highly magnified view of the iron-rich white rim. The right image is an equally extreme close-up view of the central region of the globule.

Images can be convincing, but they also can be deceiving. Although these two images closely resemble fossilized bacterial colonies on Earth, there is a major difference. Earth bacteria are generally about 100 times larger than these structures.

Because of that extreme difference in size, scientists are reluctant to call these forms fossilized microbes. Recent discoveries on Earth may change that. Deep beneath the Columbia River, within a type of igneous rock called basalt, scientists have found evidence of bacterial life as tiny as the egg-shaped and tubular structures in the Martian stone.

9

DO OTHER MARTIAN METEORITES SHOW SIGNS OF LIFE?

What could be more exciting
than finding evidence of ancient life
on Mars? Only one thing, most
meteoriticists would say: finding
evidence of recent life on Mars!

Meteorite EETA 79001 was the first Antarctic rock positively identified as being from Mars. ⬆ Of the dozen known chunks of Mars on Earth, it is the most recently formed. Radioactive dating measurements indicate that it is 180 million years old and was ejected from Mars only 600,000 years ago.

Using the same time comparison as in Chapter 4 (for the impact that launched meteorite ALH 84001 toward Earth), 600,000 years is as recent as yesterday. If Mars were twelve years old, then meteorite EETA 79001 would have formed only six months ago and would have been on Mars until only twelve hours ago. If it shows fossil evidence of bacterial life, similar bugs may well still live on Mars today.

As you read on page 41, early studies found PAHs in EETA 79001; but scientists later discovered that those may have been due to earthly contamination. Now studies of a different kind once again point to the possibility of life in that young rock. This time the evidence is in its carbonates.

You read earlier that radioactive atoms of an element have different masses from nonradioactive ones. Just as human families can be large, most elements have several isotopes of differing masses, some radioactive and others not.

In nature, C^{12} is the most common isotope of carbon. Of every thousand carbon atoms, 989 of them are C^{12}. The remaining eleven are the slightly heavier C^{13}. (Another isotope, radioactive C^{14}, also exists, but is rare. It has a relatively brief half-life of 5,700 years and is useful for measuring the age of matter that was part of a living organism within the last 20,000 years or so.)

Scientists have found that living (or once-living) matter has a somewhat different carbon composition from other natural carbon. For example, coal, which formed from ancient plant life, has more C^{12} and less C^{13} than normal carbon. The chemical processes of life work slightly better with the lighter isotope, so more C^{12} and less C^{13} finds its way into living things and their fossils.

Measurements of the carbon isotopes in the carbonates of EETA 79001 show a lower than normal C^{13} content. Scientists know of no chemical process, other than life, that might have caused such a reduction.

Much more research still needs to be done. The measurements of carbon isotopes in EETA 79001 need to be confirmed, and similar measurements must be made in other rocks from Mars and elsewhere.

Scientists must also continue their search for other chemical processes that might reduce the amount of C^{13} in a sample. That's normal scientific caution at work.

Although scientists still have no explanation except life for those low C^{13} measurements, they must not jump to the conclusion that there is no other explanation at all.

10

ISN'T MARS TOO COLD AND DRY FOR LIFE?

The weather on Mars is unearthly, to say the least! The upper image shows Mars as it looks today, a frigid, rocky desert with very little atmosphere. Yet it wasn't always that way. The same Martian landscape may have once looked like the lower image, with snow-capped mountains, glaciers, lakes, rivers, and oceans.

Its atmosphere, consisting mostly of carbon dioxide, was once thick enough to trap the warmth of the abundant sunlight–a bit less than half of what Earth receives. It had plenty of liquid water on its surface and water vapor in its atmosphere. Its weather was probably not very different from Earth's. Conditions were right for life to emerge, and the evidence from meteorite ALH 84001 suggests that it did.

Perhaps if Mars were larger–its diameter (the distance between its poles) is about half of Earth's, and its mass is only about one-tenth of our planet's–things would have been different there. Complex life forms–plants and animals–might have had the chance to develop. But the planet's small size and mass mean that its gravity is weak, about a third of ours. Over billions of years, the planet's atmosphere and water escaped the weak gravity and flowed into space.

The atmosphere of Mars is now too thin to keep the planet warm and wet. The only water on its surface is in permanent ice caps at the planet's north and south poles, where it gets so cold in winter (as much as 123 degrees below zero Celsius or 253 below zero Fahrenheit) that the air freezes and drifts to the ground as snowflakes of "dry ice." The rest of the planet's water is trapped as ice, hundreds of meters beneath the surface.

Along its equator–the hottest spot on the planet, the temperature averages 60 degrees below zero Celsius (or 76 below zero Fahrenheit). It only gets above the freezing point of water on an occasional summer day in the "tropical" latitudes, when the Sun passes nearly overhead.

How do we know that the Martian climate was once much more like Earth's? Scientists study photographs taken by spacecraft. We

see structures that look very similar to the forms created on Earth by rivers, glaciers, and huge floods.

❡ The photograph on the left is a Canadian lake that was formed in the crater left by an impact of a meteor or a comet. The photograph on the right shows a similar crater on Mars and the dry beds of its slow-moving inlet stream (upper right) and its rapid outflow (left).

With thousands of photos and years of analysis, scientists now know that Mars had periods of Earth-like climate for most of its history. The most recent may have been only 300 million years ago, when the first land animals had begun to emerge from Earth's prehistoric seas.

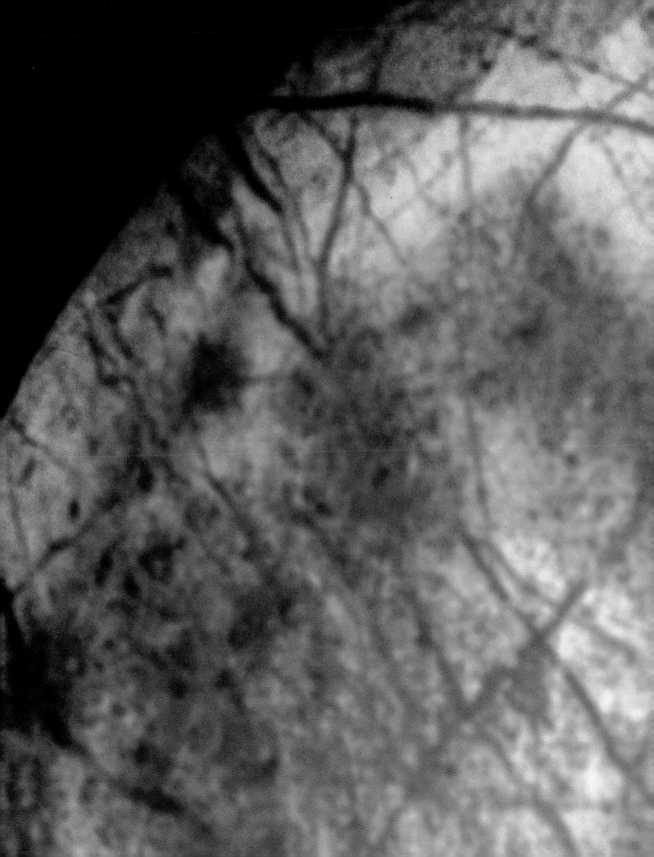

11

WHAT DO THESE FINDINGS SUGGEST ABOUT LIFE IN THE UNIVERSE?

The discovery of possible fossils in meteorite ALH 84001 has opened many exciting questions. Perhaps the most enticing is this: Does life spring up naturally wherever the environment is right? If so, then what living wonders might exist in the waters of the global ocean beneath the cracked ice surface of Europa, Jupiter's fourth-largest moon?

When the Voyager space probes of the 1970s produced spectacular images of Jupiter and its satellites, Europa became the favorite place for scientists to look for life elsewhere in the solar system. The temperature and chemical environment of Europa's ocean are suitable for life. The discovery of past life on Mars—if indeed that is what has been found—increases the likelihood of finding life on Europa.

Are there other places in the solar system to look for life? In the early history of the solar system, the Sun was cooler and the planet Venus may have been more suitable for life than Earth. Although the surface of Venus is hot enough to melt aluminum today, parts of the planet's clouds are cool enough for life as we know it. Might we find living organisms there? Not likely, say most scientists. Still, with the findings from ALH 84001, that question does not seem quite as outrageous as it once did.

Most astronomers believe that planetary systems are very common. The universe contains billions of galaxies, and each galaxy contains billions of stars and probably billions of planets. Surely, they say, a vast number of those planets are habitable. That means they have conditions that could support life in some form.

Many scientists say that the news from meteorite ALH 84001 means that life begins on any planet or moon where conditions are suitable. If that is so, then most habitable planets are home to living creatures. The natural phenomena that led to complex life on Earth would lead to complex life elsewhere as well. It would be arrogant for us humans to believe that of all the life forms on all the planets of all the galaxies, we are the most intelligent and powerful that ever existed.

Certainly, human life—and all other life on our planet—is a wonder. Even more wondrous is that intelligent beings, like us in many ways and different in many others, probably exist throughout the vast universe. On planets scattered among the galaxies, young beings like you may be reading books. Those books might be about recent discoveries from other planets. Could those discoveries, like the findings in meteorite ALH 84001, change the way those young creatures think of their species, their planet, and life in the universe?

Think about how scientific observation has led us to change our views of those subjects here on Earth. Because life is a wonder, it was only natural for early civilizations to view humans as special beings living on a special world. Until the sixteenth century, most people believed that Earth was the center of the universe. Scientists who claimed otherwise were often ridiculed, and those who spoke and wrote most powerfully were severely punished.

Ultimately, the scientific evidence was overwhelming. Most people reluctantly accepted that Earth was merely one of several planets going around the Sun. Even so, they still believed we were special creatures living on a planet going around a special Sun. The Sun, they were certain, was the center of the universe, and Earth and all heavenly bodies went around it.

Gradually, people came to know that the Sun is not special after all. It is, they realized, an ordinary star. Still, they believed that humans were unlike all other creatures, and that we lived on a world unlike any other.

In the nineteenth and twentieth centuries, people began to abandon those ideas as well. We now know that our Sun is not at the center of anything other than the solar system itself. It is located near the edge of the Milky Way, an ordinary galaxy.

We also now understand that all living species on our planet developed gradually by a natural process, each adapting to its place in the world. Human beings, though gifted with intelligence and capable bodies, are made of the same substances as all the other creatures on Earth.

Nature's chemistry had created a marvelous substance known as deoxyribonucleic acid, or DNA. DNA determines whether an organism is a fungus, plant, or animal. It determines what species that organism belongs to. It determines individual characteristics of that organism. Your DNA not only makes you a person, but it makes you different (unless you have an identical twin) from every other person who ever lived. What a wonder this DNA-based human species is!

Of course, every other life form on our planet is equally wonderful. That is still hard for some people to accept. How can we ask such people to accept the idea that the universe is filled with planets as blessed as ours, inhabited by creatures at least our equal?

Perhaps we can persuade them with these awesome thoughts: Long before our Sun existed, there were probably planets with civilizations as grand as or grander than ours. Long after our Sun has cooled, the wonder of life will probably continue throughout an ever-changing universe. We are only beginning to understand and appreciate the glorious future that awaits us as living beings in a universe filled with life.

That may be the most important message hidden in the specks and flecks of meteorite ALH 84001.

12

DO ALL SCIENTISTS AGREE ABOUT THE MEANING OF THESE FINDINGS?

The title of this book, *Martian Fossils on Earth?*, ends with a question mark for good reason. The discovery of possible evidence of ancient life in a meteorite from Mars is very exciting. Still, every scientist on the team studying meteorite ALH 84001 agrees: Together, their many findings propose a theory that life existed on Mars billions of years ago, but more and stronger evidence is needed to support such a powerful claim.

When National Aeronautics and Space Administration (NASA) Administrator Daniel Goldin called a news conference to discuss those findings, he did something quite unusual. He invited a scientist who was not a member of the research team to speak. William Schopf, a highly respected planetary scientist, discussed each piece of evidence and gave alternative interpretations for some of them.

By inviting Schopf, Administrator Goldin did what every scientist should. He subjected the evidence to serious criticism. Scientists believe a theory only after they have done everything they can to discredit it. The more criticism it survives, the more believable it becomes.

Schopf admitted that the NASA researchers' evidence might be due to ancient Martian life. But he added, in the words of famous astronomer and author Carl Sagan, "Extraordinary claims require extraordinary evidence." The discovery of Martian fossils is a most extraordinary claim, indeed.

Schopf said that he needed to be convinced of seven points before he could recognize the evidence as extraordinary. Four dealt with the rock itself. Where did it come from? How old is it? In what kind of environment did it form? What is its history?

The other three points dealt with the presumed fossil evidence. First, are they really within the rock? Second, are they as old as the rock? Third, "are they demonstrably, assuredly, certainly biological?"

He discussed these questions one at a time. Where did the rock come from? He agreed that it was most likely from Mars. On a scale ranging from one to ten, he gave it a nine.

He was also fairly confident about the history of the meteorite as well. He specifically discussed the age claimed for the carbonates, about 3.6 billion years. "That's a little more uncertain," he said. "I give that a confidence rating of eight. But I think that's pretty good stuff."

What about the environment in which the carbonates formed? The NASA research team believed they formed in liquid water, but another team of researchers, led by scientist and author Harry Y. McSween, Jr., claim that the carbonates formed at about 450 degrees Celsius (840 degrees Fahrenheit). If that was the case, nothing could have lived within the carbonates. "I am not taking sides...," Schopf said. "I am simply saying this is not a resolved issue."

Looking at the chemicals and the structures claimed to be fossils, Schopf stated that "it has been established certainly to my satisfaction, beyond any doubt ..., that both the ... [PAHs] and the fossil-like structures occur within the rocks."

He is almost as certain that they are about as old as the carbonates in the rock. "I give it an eight or nine rating," he said.

"With regard to the biology," he continued, "I take a rather different view.... I'd say that the first guess would be that they're probably nonbiological, just like the PAHs that occur in other meteorites."

He also expressed doubt about the "fossil-like objects," as he called them. He pointed out that they are 100 times smaller than such fossils found on Earth. Because they are so small, he added, they could not be analyzed chemically. Finally, he said, there is no evidence of cell structure as would exist in a living organism.

Although he felt that the proof of ancient life was weak, he added that "it's possible to do additional science to answer these questions, to test this and move it up the confidence scale."

Schopf concluded his remarks by returning to the view offered by Carl Sagan: "Extraordinary claims require extraordinary evidence. We know the sort of evidence that we need to obtain regarding these samples. Personally, I think this is exciting. I think it's very interesting. I think they're pointing in the right direction. But I think ... a certain amount of additional work needs to be done before we can have firm confidence that this report is of life on Mars."

ARTIST'S RENDERING OF A SPACECRAFT RETURNING MARTIAN ROCKS AND SOIL TO EARTH.

13

WHAT'S NEXT ON MARS?

While one group of NASA scientists studied possible fossil life in meteorite ALH 84001, other groups around the world prepared for missions to Mars. Late 1996 saw the launching of three long-planned planetary exploration spacecraft. The final stage of the rocket carrying the Russian *Mars 96* spacecraft failed, and that hoped-for planetary laboratory, carrying experiments from several countries, fell into the Pacific Ocean.

Two United States rocket launchings were successful, and their payloads headed for mid-1997 encounters with the red planet. As this book was printed, *Mars Global Surveyor* (*MGS*) was on its way to Mars. The mission of *MGS* is to orbit the planet and, over many

months, produce detailed maps of the planet's landforms, weather, and chemical makeup. *Pathfinder,* carrying a small robot rover named *Sojourner,* ◀▪ shown here in the laboratory before launch, landed on the Martian surface on July 4, 1997. Within days, *Sojourner* began analyzing nearby rocks that scientists had given whimsical names such as "Barnacle Bill" and "Yogi." ▪▶

Because the planning of planetary missions takes many years, most of the work of those two spacecraft was laid out long before anyone knew of possible Martian fossils on Earth. Now those missions take on added significance. Scientists will carefully study *MGS* maps for possible landing sites for future fossil-hunting or life-seeking missions. They will examine *Pathfinder*'s data for signs of life, even though its experiments were not designed primarily for that purpose.

Every two years, when Earth and Mars are properly aligned for other missions, additional spacecraft will follow. Many will carry scientific instruments to follow up on the initial *MGS* and *Pathfinder* discoveries. Through those missions, NASA plans to create a planet-wide network of small chemical probes, weather stations, and seismographs (used to measure earthquakes).

Within ten years, perhaps even as early as 2005, NASA hopes to return a collection of Martian rocks and soil to Earth. Perhaps one of those rocks will confirm the theory that Martian microbes once lived in meteorite ALH 84001.

After that, the next step is to send humans to Mars. NASA's Apollo program proved that we can send people to another world and bring them back safely. It also demonstrated that human eyes and minds are far more valuable for planetary exploration than robots can ever be.

In 1996, Astronaut Shannon Lucid set a record by spending more than six months in orbit aboard U. S. space shuttles and the Russian space station *Mir*. She returned home in excellent physical condition. Had she spent those six months traveling to Mars, she would have arrived ready and able to go to work.

When will people go to Mars? Before scientists found possible fossils in meteorite ALH 84001, the answer to that question was, "Probably not until we have a good reason to send them." Now the answer is, "Probably by 2025; possibly much earlier."

The Apollo missions to the Moon ended in December 1972, only three and a half years after the first human landing there. Human missions to Mars will probably continue much longer than that. Most scientists speak of setting up a permanent base on Mars similar to scientific stations on Antarctica. Chances are excellent that many of the young people reading this book–perhaps you–will compete for the opportunity to live on Mars for a year or more.

If you go, you and your fellow pioneers will arrive on Mars loaded with questions. You will return home, like all the scientists and explorers before you, with many more.

AUTHOR'S NOTE

Often a book like this has a list of other books on the subject. I thought about including one, but I had a problem: There are no other books on the subject.

This is the first book for young readers about Meteorite ALH 84001. I know of one adult book about the meteorite that will appear before this one (*The Hunt for Life on Mars* by Donald Goldsmith), but that book was not published when I wrote these words. Although I plan to read it, I never recommend a book I haven't seen.

This book is about questions rather than answers. If I did my job, you will want to ask your own questions as new scientific discoveries are announced. How can you do that? The best way is to use the same types of sources that I did: magazines and the World Wide Web. You can find a good magazine collection in most libraries. Many, if not most, libraries now are connected to the "information superhighway." Librarians are glad to show you how to find magazine articles, old and new, on any topic, and how to explore the World Wide Web.

Whenever I write a book, I am always concerned about using the most current and accurate information I can find. The Web is full of information, but not all of it can be trusted. Still, to write on a topic as "hot" as Meteorite ALH 84001, the Web was my most important source of news releases, images, and pointers to the latest scientific results.

As an experienced researcher, I know how to make sure the information I find on the Web is valid. If you decide to explore the Web, I recommend starting with the Mars Meteorite Home Page (http://www.jpl.nasa.gov/snc) from the Jet Propulsion Laboratory. You can follow its links to many great images of ALH 84001 and other Martian meteorites, to news releases, and to articles in newspapers, magazines, and scientific journals.

GLOSSARY

Allan Hills: The region of Antarctica in which Meteorite ALH 84001 was discovered.

ANSMET: The Antarctic Search for Meteorites project, which discovered Meteorite ALH 84001.

carbonate: A chemical compound that forms in the presence of carbon dioxide and water. Meteorite ALH 84001 contains carbonate globules that may have contained living organisms.

chassignite: The name of a family of meteorites that resemble one that fell on Chassigny, France, on October 3, 1815.

crater: A large, round depression on the surface of a planet, moon, or smaller body. On planets and moons, craters are often signs of impacts of meteorites or larger bodies from space.

daughter nucleus: A particular type of nucleus that results from the radioactive decay of another type of nucleus known as its parent.

diogenite: A particular class of meteorite. ALH 84001 was at first misidentified as a diogenite meteorite, and thus not from Mars.

Europa: A moon of the planet Jupiter that may have a global liquid-water ocean under an icy crust. In future space probes, scientists may look for life in that ocean.

fossil: A structure in a rock that preserves the appearance of an organism that lived when the rock was forming.

fusion crust: The smooth, usually black outer region of a meteorite that forms when its surface, melted by intense heat as it passes through the atmosphere, solidifies again.

globule: A small object having a rounded shape. Meteorite ALH 84001 had globules of carbonate material in its cracks.

greigite: A form of iron sulfide often produced on Earth by organisms living in the soil. Meteorite ALH 84001 contains crystals of iron sulfide that may be greigite and have shapes similar to those produced by bacteria on Earth.

half-life: The period of time in which half of a particular kind of radioactive parent nuclei will decay into their daughter nuclei. After one half-life, half of the original nuclei remains; after two half-lives, only half of those—or one-fourth of the original number remain; and so forth.

igneous: A type of rock that forms from the cooling of magma. Meteorite ALH 84001 is an igneous rock.

isotope: A particular form of an atomic nucleus having a particular mass. The number of protons in the nucleus determines what type of atom it is, and the total number of protons and neutrons determines its mass. Oxygen nuclei contain eight protons and either eight, nine, or ten neutrons; so oxygen has three common isotopes, designated O^{16}, O^{17}, and O^{18}.

magma: Hot liquid rock that, when cooled, becomes igneous rock. Magma still exists in great chambers within Earth. Magma was once common on Mars, but it is now rare or nonexistent there.

magnetite: A magnetic form of iron oxide. Some bacteria on Earth create tiny crystals of magnetite. The carbonate globules of Meteorite ALH 84001 contain magnetite crystals that some scientists think may have been produced by Martian organisms.

Mars 96: A 1996 Russian spacecraft that failed to go into space for its planned exploration of Mars.

Mars Global Surveyor (MGS): A United States spacecraft that was launched in late 1996 and is scheduled to orbit Mars and produce detailed maps of its landforms, weather, and chemical makeup beginning in 1997.

meteor: A glowing streak of light across the sky caused by the heating of a rapidly moving piece of matter from outer space as it strikes a planet's or moon's atmosphere. Although people usually use this word to describe a phenomenon on Earth, meteors can occur on any body that has an atmosphere.

meteorite: A stone or rock from outer space that has fallen to the surface of a planet, moon, or other large body. Usually, people normally think of meteorites on Earth, but they can land on any substantial body, including an asteroid.

meteoriticist: A scientist who studies meteorites.

mineral: A particular chemical with a particular crystal structure found in rocks.

Mir: The orbiting Russian space station, in which astronauts and cosmonauts have lived and maintained their physical strength for long periods of time, proving that humans have the capability to go to Mars, work there, and return home.

nakhlite: The name of a family of meteorites that resemble one that fell on Nakhla, Egypt, on June 28, 1911, killing a dog.

neutron: One of two types of small particles that make up the nucleus of an atom, the other type being the proton.

nucleus (plural: **nuclei**): The central part of an atom, containing protons and neutrons.

orbit: The path of a planet, moon, or smaller body around a larger one, such as Earth's orbit around the Sun or the Moon's around Earth.

parent nucleus: A particular type of nucleus that will, upon radioactive decay, transform into another type of nucleus known as its daughter.

Pathfinder: A United States spacecraft that landed on Mars on July 4, 1997, carrying the roving robotic lander *Sojourner* to explore and take measurements of a small portion of the planet's surface.

polycyclic aromatic hydrocarbon (**PAH**): One of a certain class of chemical compounds of carbon and hydrogen that may be a sign of life. Some scientists believe that PAHs found in or near the carbonate globules of Meteorite ALH 84001 may have been produced by ancient Martian organisms.

proton: One of two types of small particles that make up the nucleus of an atom, the other type being the neutron. The number of protons determines what type of atom it is.

radioactive dating: A technique that uses measurements of parent and daughter nuclei and the half-life of a particular radioactive decay to determine how long ago a particular event happened to a particular object. Different parent-daughter combinations enabled scientists to determine when Meteorite ALH 84001 formed, when it developed cracks, when carbonate globules formed in those cracks, when it was blasted from the Martian surface, how long it took to reach Earth, and how long it lay in Antarctica before it was discovered.

radioactive decay: A process in which a nucleus, known as the parent, transforms into another, known as the daughter. Each particular radioactive decay proceeds at a distinct rate, measured by its half-life or the interval of time in which half of the parent nuclei will undergo the transformation.

shergottite: The name of a family of meteorites that resembles one that fell on Shergotty, India, on August 25, 1865. Meteorite ALH 84001 is a shergottite meteorite.

SNC: The class of meteorites consisting of shergottites, nakhlites, and chassignites.

Sojourner: A roving robotic lander carried aboard the United States spacecraft, *Pathfinder*, that landed on Mars on July 4, 1997. *Sojourner* explored and took measurements of a small portion of the planet's surface.

solar system: The sun and all the bodies orbiting around it, including the planets, their moons, asteroids, comets, and many tiny pieces of matter.

solar wind: A stream of high energy particles that flow outward from the Sun. While Meteorite ALH 84001 traveled from Mars to Earth, the solar wind transformed some of its nuclei into radioactive ones, enabling scientists to determine how long that trip lasted and how long ago it ended.

transmission electron microscope (TEM): A powerful magnifying machine that produces images of thin slices of an object. TEM images of the carbonate globules in Meteorite ALH 84001 revealed magnetite and greigite crystals.

trapped-gas analysis: A technique in which scientists determine the mixture of gases trapped in a rock or soil sample. Trapped gas analysis of SNC meteorites provides strong evidence that they came from Mars.

INDEX